S0-CTH-451

Growing Readers

Purchased with Smart Start Funds

POLICE STATIONS

GREAT PLACES TO VISIT

Jason Cooper

The Rourke Corporation, Inc.
Vero Beach, Florida 32964

NEW HANOVER COUNTY
PUBLIC LIBRARY
201 CHESTNUT STREET
WILMINGTON, NC 28401

© 1992 The Rourke Corporation, Inc.

All rights reserved. No part of this book
may be reproduced or utilized in any form
or by any means, electronic or mechanical
including photocopying, recording or by
any information storage and retrieval
system without permission in writing from
the publisher.

Edited by Sandra A. Robinson

PHOTO CREDITS
© Lynn M. Stone: All photos

ACKNOWLEDGEMENTS
The author thanks the following for their cooperation in the
preparation of this book: City of Aurora, IL, Police Department; City
of Batavia, IL, Police Department

LIBRARY OF CONGRESS
Library of Congress Cataloging-in-Publication Data
Cooper, Jason, 1942-
   Police stations / Jason Cooper.
     p. cm. — (Great places to visit)
   Includes index.
   ISBN 0-86593-213-1
   1. Police—Juvenile literature. 2. Police—United States—
Juvenile literature. I. Title. II. Series: Cooper, Jason, 1942-
Great places to visit.
HV7922.C67   1992
363.2'0973—dc20   92-12575
                               CIP
                                AC

Printed in the USA

TABLE OF CONTENTS

Police Stations   5
Police Officers   6
Detectives   9
The Police Officer's Job   11
Working in the Police Station   14
Suspects   16
The Jail and Police Lab   19
Police Equipment   20
Police Programs   22
Glossary   23
Index   24

POLICE STATIONS

When you visit a city police station, you will meet men and women wearing blue uniforms—police officers.

The police station is the building where police officers report for work.

Police officers help protect people and property. They do that by enforcing laws that governments make.

City, county and state governments each hire police officers who make up a police department.

Officer showing handcuffs to third graders

POLICE OFFICERS

You may not see many officers at the station. Most police will be out, working in the community.

Police officers have certain areas to visit, or patrol, each day. Most of these areas, called **beats,** are visited by car. But some beats are patrolled on foot or from horseback.

Police officer by squad car

DETECTIVES

You will see police officers in uniform. You may also see officers whom you do not recognize as police. That is because they are **detectives.** Detectives are also called plainclothes officers because they do not wear police uniforms.

Detectives work to solve and prevent **crimes,** serious actions that are against the law. They do not work a beat, as many uniformed police officers do.

Detective at his desk

THE POLICE OFFICER'S JOB

Police officers perform many services, and some of them are quite dangerous. They answer calls from people who are in danger and assist them. They search for people who are involved in crimes and capture them. They also help to keep traffic running smoothly and assist at accidents.

In the station, you will see several rooms where police work.

Police officer reviewing a list of stolen property

Police officers planning a traffic patrol

Visitor learns how fingerprints are taken

WORKING IN THE POLICE STATION

In the **dispatch,** or message, room, a dispatcher uses a radio to direct a police officer to someone who needs help.

The station's records room keeps information about old and new police cases in files and computers.

Officer work areas are set up to help police take care of record-keeping when they return from their beats.

Police station dispatch room
alerts police on patrol to trouble

SUSPECTS

Someone who may have committed a crime is a **suspect.** Police officers often question suspects at the station. Sometimes a suspect is **arrested** in the booking room, where officers can check a book to see exactly with what a suspect should be charged.

Someone who is arrested has been charged by the police with doing something against the law. In cases of serious crimes, a suspect may have to be jailed even before the case goes to trial in a courtroom.

Jail cells in a city police station

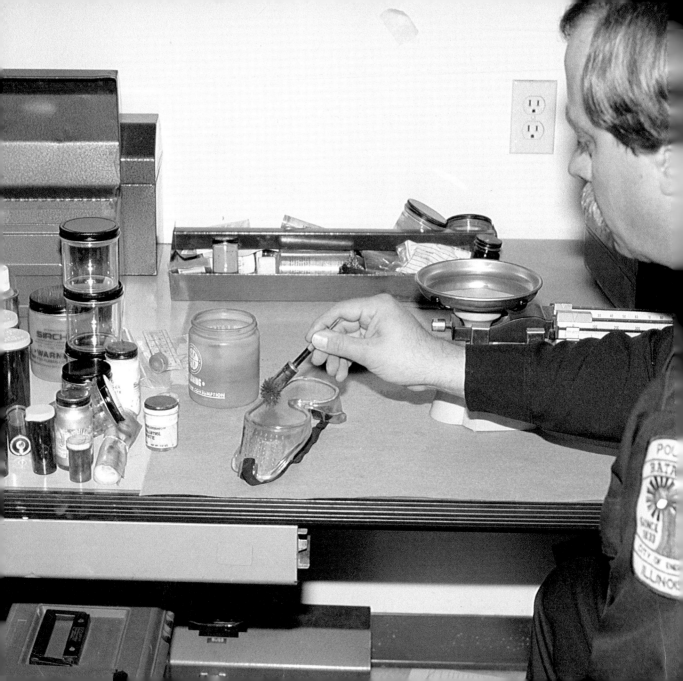

THE JAIL AND POLICE LAB

The city police station's jail is used to keep prisoners for a short time. People charged with serious crimes are usually sent to larger jails.

At the station **laboratory** you will see equipment used to conduct many different kinds of tests, such as fingerprint tests.

Labs help police collect **evidence.** Evidence proves what really happened.

Labs also examine substances to decide what they are and to whom they belong.

Police officer in station laboratory

POLICE EQUIPMENT

Police officers carry equipment that helps them to protect themselves and other people. Police officers carry a two-way radio, handcuffs, a pistol, bullets and a club. Some officers wear bulletproof vests.

Police officers drive automobiles know as squad cars. Police also have **"paddy wagons,"** which are vans used to transport prisoners.

Standard police equipment on an officer's belt

POLICE PROGRAMS

Police officers conduct educational programs for students, teachers and the general public. Officers visit homes, schools and organizations. They also bring groups of young people to the police station.

A police program being used throughout North America is Drug Abuse Resistance Education, known as D.A.R.E. This program warns young people of the dangers of using unlawful drugs. It also dares them to say "No!" to drugs.

Glossary

arrested (uh REST ed) — charged with a crime or breaking the law

beat (BEET) — a regular route or area to be visited

crime (KRIME) — a serious act that is against the law

detective (de TEKT ihv) — a plainclothes police officer specializing in criminal cases

dispatch (DIS pahtsh) — a message

evidence (EHV uh dense) — a body of collected facts and materials that helps prove something, such as someone's guilt or innocence

laboratory (LAB rah tor ee) — a working area in which various tests can be carried out under controlled conditions

paddy wagon (PAH dee WAG un) — a police vehicle, like a van, used to carry prisoners of police

suspect (SUS pehkt) — one who has been accused or charged with a crime

INDEX

accidents   11
beats   6, 9
courtroom   16
crimes   9, 11, 16
detectives   9
dispatch room   14
Drug Abuse Resistance Education
    (D.A.R.E.)   22
evidence   19
fingerprints   19
governments   5
handcuffs   22
jail   19
laboratory   19
paddy wagons   22

pistol   22
plainclothes officers   9
police department   5
police officers   5, 6, 9,
    11, 14, 16, 20, 22
prisoners   19, 22
programs   20
radio, two-way   22
records   14
squad cars   22
suspects   16
traffic   11
vest, bulletproof   22

Growing Readers
New Hanover County
Public Library
201 Chestnut Street
Wilmington, NC 28401